Salt and Petals

James Milenkovic

Salt and Petals

Acknowledgements

I humbly give thanks to Caitilin Punshon for her perceptive comments, and offering me support and guidance during the shaping of this collection. I also thank Chris Elmore for his kind words. I extend my appreciation to the spectacular team at Ginninderra Press, who have afforded me this fabulous opportunity, especially Stephen Matthews. Thanks also to Gabriele De Palma who produced the ethereal front cover design, Eternity. Moreover, I thank the subjects of these poems for sparking something within me (be they anonymous or not). Also, I humbly thank you, the reader, for investing your time in this collection.

Finally, my dear family – Mum, Jode and Bec – who have encouraged me, supported me, challenged me and loved me through this journey. I love you all.

For Mum, Jode and Bec

Salt and Petals
ISBN 978 1 76041 073 5
Copyright © text James Milenkovic 2016
Cover: Gabriele De Palma

First published 2016 by
Ginninderra Press
PO Box 3461 Port Adelaide 5015 Australia
www.ginninderrapress.com.au

Contents

Under a Banner of Sun	7
Country Victoria	9
Rabbit	12
Retaking	13
The Hill	14
Creek	16
Crash	17
Development	19
Peak Hour Train	20
Kite	22
Summer Storm	23
Out the Window	25
Into the Pearled Space	27
Opal, Coober Pedy	29
Pauline	30
Restless	31
Inferior	32
Shoes	33
Pub Men	34
Road Kill	36
Youth Den	37
Forces	38
Spare Room	39
After Rain	40
First Snow, August 2014	41
Beach at Night	42
The Lamplight of Our Existence	43
Earliest Morning	45
Beehive	46

Learning Oil Painting	47
Planting	48
Dinner, Devour, Dachshund	49
Lost	50
Hospice	51
That Day, Winter '04	53
Alone	54
Overawe	55
Passing Through	56
Tenterhooks	57
Umbrella Bells	58
The Boy With Two Sugars in His Tea	59
New Home	61
Lasik	62
The Trembling Flame	**63**
Hummingbird	65
Depression, 2012	66
Fever	67
I Do Not Miss You	68
Eyes	69
Insomnia	70
Awake	71
Spider's Web	72
Rose and Thorn	73
Metamorphosis	74
Tattoo	75
Scars	76
Hands	77
Candle	78
Beyond This	79

Under a Banner of Sun

Country Victoria

i Driving

we packed up the comforts of home
to vacate for the weekend,
heading into the trappings
                               of country living:
slumberous hamlets of wood fires, loam and livestock

we drive through a curling lip
of road,
ablaze with yellow, orange and red –
coming into an expanse
                               of countryside
beneath a cupola of cerulean,
barrels of hay lie like pieces of roulade
         adjacent fields of glowing canola, and the paternal
watching
of ancient mountains.

ii Woolshed

nestled amid an outcropping of
pines –
        their scent syrupy and unmistakable –
the deeply-rooted frame of the woolshed,
        its jacket of wooden laths decaying,
stands below triangular slats
of oxidised iron

to think this barn was once   busy
with operation –
the lugging back and forth of sheep,
        the buzz of shearing clippers,
horse and cart collecting the labours of brawny men
is hard to ponder,
though,
this sward has recently been clipped, and a fence pail –
newer than its compatriots –
has been replaced by   somebody

the byre has since gone quiet,
left to the landscape and the abrading attention
of wind, rain and sun.

iii Macedon Ranges History

Spirit songs are heard
through tree
     and creek,
ancient practices performed
   under a banner of sun   and
starlight

this land,
with its grassy waterways
       and mountain ridges,
  is where the Elder
whisper legends,
eternally communing
   history and story
through channels of earth
     to the heeding ear.

Rabbit

Under the canopied foliage at Mt Macedon
one amorphous creature flits and flitters,
scouring the surrounds like a
        curious child

long feet grounded
and pointed ears twitch while
scrutinising eyes   dart about,
trying to demystify what hides in
the masking haze

I watch – intent – from the bench,
hatted and coated against the bitter
morning chill and time spent watching
this creature;
sharp beats of icy air filling my lungs

and just like that,
the rabbit bounds through
brush in a smoky flash,
passing over and under,
weaving between its cordons,
unnerved yet
quiet,
disappearing into the vapour like a spirit

Retaking

See how these settlements we've built
for our urban human occupation,
draining   forms of earth,
are again being reclaimed   by the patient
triumph of land, plant and animal:

a procession of bricks
rectangular and metrical
has been beleaguered by a circulatory tangle
of tree roots,
        tunnelling through and over their sidewalk plots
enveloping the ground with a tousling blanket
                of earthly victory,

civilised spots   becoming wild zones
that quickly eradicate any suggestion
of our
        temporary
        dependent
                existence.

The Hill

The Hill is the name given to foreboding buildings atop Jacksons Hill in Sunbury, a small town approximately 40 kilometres from Melbourne. During its 150 years, the site has served as an industrial school, a women's reformatory, a mental asylum and a Victoria University campus. Though now abandoned and constantly vandalised, the history and energy of the site are palpable.

They lingered
here
on this tor of green
pared now with shrub and floret,
naked in merciless westerlies
                      and tortured
with grievance

Their voiceless memories
interred in the red bricks
scattered arbitrarily o'er the crest,
                      nefarious but beautiful,
ethereal bodies leaving an auric stain of
sickness

solemn vestiges observed now
through crusted windows,
inert and cold lives
       refracted
to those careful enough to look
without ministering hands,
mobs continue to proffer destruction.

How can it be that
even in death, no light,
no repose
suffuses
        their darkness?

Creek

in the tired morning of earthy perfume and smoke
(not even sunup),
the nomad drives across the interfold of creek and dipping range,
following the fossilised carvings from his many trips
up to the high country.

The creek's swelled with the triumph of rain,
bank brimming to the mesh of serrated tussock and weeds
      spearing through the mire,
its refilling calling frogs and birds back
           with sentient promise.

In disbelief,
he gets out of his four-wheel drive and listens
to the music of the scooping boule:
the swishing of ashy grasses in the saccharine air,
      an orchestra of cockatoos screeching
from the gnarly arms of pines,
trickling
through unseen intersections of terrain and body
and disappearing
           into the allaying shroud of dawn.

Crash

The road turns sharply
and the car is   somehow   bucked,
thrown
off the familiarity of road
and tossed toy-like and flimsy
down the embankment,
        furious sound
                pounding
eyes snap shut,
hands on wheel tighten,
      waiting,
               holding   breathing

I clamber out from this graveyard of
wrangled metal,
        twisted and crumpled piles
of metallic nothingness
      my body heavy and
                still
in the clutches of numbing shock,
a torrent of confusion

a sudden pain,
I clasp hand to head and feel
the clamminess of blood,
        violent, red wound;

a driver's pulled over,
        rushing down the levee
calling something

the familiarity of another person,
a promise of imminent help,
calls me back to the present moment,
the wreckage,
the thin band of sun on my cheek,
        shallow breath of life,
how lucky I am.

Development

Not too long ago
there was a hillside proximate my house,
vast and proud in its green
loveliness.
        Cows grazed unflappably on its mantle,
peppered with grass and buttercup,
abutted by early morning cloud
                before the rushing triumph of dawn.

Soon,
metallic leviathans took to this prairie, implacably,
        exhuming soil and rock,
leaving serpentine tracks and
                the effluence of
        sirens and
                manufacturing

Soon
        wooden bones,
                bricked assemblages encroached
this hitherto pictorial mount,
replicating,

        up and up until
my mountain was desecrated.

Peak Hour Train

Umbrellas aloft,
held like beacons of sanguinity
in the bleakness of the early morning:
        vexed travellers wait, sleekly dressed
(surely uncomfortable in the damp
and at what time did they wake to prepare?)

An apparition of light – wraithlike –
perforates the mélange of rain and haze,
the Metro train,
        its tubular body barely distinguishable
screeches to a halt

We move as a mass, taking strident steps
towards the hiss of opening doors
then
we unfasten
violently spilling through the entrance,
        moving
(heedless of slipperiness)
        pushing through clambering
passengers to secure a seat

The morning commute is the place of convergence,
anonymous nomads aggregated
by look and conversation   and purpose
until
we terminate,
again to
        scatter
and depart,
                stepping into the grey expanse of the city,
        becoming indistinguishable drops
in the rain.

Kite

Walking through the park I see two boys
flying a yellow kite,
its long red streamer swaying and
flapping
in the brisk current;

I hear it tugging against the string,
thin judders of sound
something of a forewarning
as the boys begin to squabble
over who orchestrates the airborne
body.

The petulant exchange turns
to wild rumpus,
        and in the moment of dispute
the kite's handle abandons
the boy's hands and
drags   over manicured lawn
        until the nylon skin is hoisted,

                                            up

and over, and
        away,
the tether from earth to sky
                is broken.

Summer Storm

Heat wave. Tenth day over thirty.
The fan tiredly humming,
torrents of cool
               (not cold) air
bob between the blinds.
The prevailing light strikes the television with crisp linearity;
taste of metallic heat outside,
baking brick and bitumen.

Lying on the couch,
        skin sticking to the tessellated fabric weaves;
with a sleeping dog moulding himself around
my form,
too hot to gnaw a bone.

Rush of ice and water
        swills the cavity of my mouth
bringing stint of sharp,
        all-consuming
               pain,
then sweetly numbing relief,
        some semblance of homeostasis

The blue tongue might come out today,
skulk through the leafy jumble
        onto the patio, or
the fires from Whittlesea could gorge
on bleached grass and dusty eucalypt:
roaming   snakelike,
across the husky paddock.

But instead the storm's come early:
grey layers mélange and
churn in the massiveness of the sky,
languid faces turn upwards,
exultant
as the first
drop
                                        falls.

Out the Window

It seems that again I find myself
        staring out of the paned window

becoming hermetical in what was
once my calm home,
        lost somewhere
        in its interstitial spaces,
amid an unravelling of threads,
with no needle   no hand adept enough
        to darn it back

The light
              of early morning commute
              manifests through the drawing back of
curtains
        coffee run before the 9 a.m. meeting,
the carving of streets
        in the early winter day

If I pity them, why then am I envious?
If I'm so happy here   why can't I think of anything
                          but getting   out?

Into the Pearled Space

Opal, Coober Pedy

Equipped with headlamp, chisel
and hammer
we journey down
the carved labyrinth of mine,
far below the plateau of gingery sand and
baking sun,
hoping to find a streak of
rainbow   somewhere in the rock face:

our blunt and jagged swiping reveals
a kaleidoscopic river
                        running,
               like veins through the body of rock

it's a onerous process –
silica liquescence filling crevice and void
over and again,
                   eventually coagulating
granting a panoply
      of light and brilliance.

Pauline

I hate to think of my grandmother alone,
locked away
in her two-bedroom unit,
days spent
                chair-bound,
watching old movies
       and ruminating
over bygone annals,
utterly bored with the tedium
       of daily routine.

We visit when we can,
dismayed to see the woman
whose graceful company I loved as a child,
                                      now in hermitage:
divorced from the timbre of conversation
(Pop calling you Bink),
the familiarity of serving tea to company –

In the absence of immigrating
back to your former life,
I hope that our visits, or the prospect
of being returned to him
is enough
       to conciliate the burden of your loneliness.

Restless

In the black wholeness of the bedroom
(except for the pastel tang of a night light)
a restless child lurches
and heaves –
pulling
        sliding
inside their vessel
to slumber

blankets not fully covering,
pillow – unplumped – not rightly cradling head,
        arid throat craving water

the child calls
across the infinity of the black room
to the light dwellers on the other
                                      side.

'On the next ad' answers Mum,
but it's too long for the child to wait:
already the monsters are emerging from the nebulous black,
advancing across the nocturnal pasture,

advancing.

Inferior

The glossy poster of an impressive specimen –
the manliness of his unsheathed form –
of rippling muscle and pronounced contour,
reminds me that my body,
so different to his, will not,
        cannot,
exhibit the garment as he does.

I hear the click-clock of stilettos approaching –
'Can I help you with anything?' the shop assistant asks
'No thanks, I'm just browsing,' I say
and I am filled with the immediate need to get out,
        ashamed

Can I (by buying this
        overpriced fabric,
worn by this nameless man)
too be made admirable by passers-by?
Am I revealing the best of me
By covering myself?

I leave promptly,
avoiding my reflection in the mirror
and the static gaze of that engineered male,
who has with such ease
        eclipsed whatever faith I once had
in my suddenly,
        patently,
inferior body.

Shoes

peddlers make the final preparations
before the parsimonious
descend upon the stores, like flies to dead flesh:
      rummaging,
             annexing to find the pickings
of value:

I find – obfuscated behind bric-a-brac –
a pair of shoes, sister to some I have slumped
             in the dungeon of my walk-in wardrobe

curious

no scuff is rendered on this specimen before me,
      the apple of its heel, glossy,
its stitching uniform.
How has it found
its home   amongst the debris
                  of others' lives?

Pub Men

Walking down the street I hear
the terse exchange of a macho chorus
                          up ahead,
between blokes sitting, pride-like beneath an expanse of
umbrella shade
        outside the pub,
lazing in the fading opalescent hours of the hot
summer day

I am inclined to reroute my journey,
cross the quiet street to
go 'round the rabble of beer-guzzlers and
discomforting natter,
        hoping
        to bypass the likely
                disdain of these burly beasts,
from being the night's pickings for the pack

This gangling body,
        the angularity of my face
and pallid tone of skin –
        visceral indexes of my being:
              who I love, what attracts me –
                      so dissimilar to them;

but how am I less a man than they? –
we are not so far removed
        by blade of flesh
                and the coursing of testosterone –

why do I care anyway?
when did I let myself become unnerved,
so tractable?

I walk past them.

Road Kill

The body of the Eastern Grey is sprawled
across the road's edge,
        freshly struck.
        Its fleece unfurled   mangled tissue
shiny
with clotting blood –
        spoiled under the banner of
                      morning sun.
Murder of crows,
        ebony and glossy,
sniff out the find,
        sink black talons into its flesh,
to pick
        and pull apart
        rubbery and exposed guttings –

a slow devouring of the laughing brutes.

Youth Den

In the black hole of the warren

empty bottles and cigarette butts follow
along puddled concrete with

the flickering of candles and the thunder
of heavy metal;

the silky curve of the new girl's skin,
her obliging promise of surrender

now red and blue resound in the dark:
fleeing wild creatures in the night.

Forces

The rain is still

falling
hours now without reprieve
heavy and hard into
the churning spill of stream,
the dispersing torrent of rage

(meanwhile, we take refuge indoors,
drying off by

a whispering fire)
catching in the cratered diverts of
gutter and garden,
while its silvery violence wreaks havoc;

it stirs within me the swell
of dark excitement, approbation

powerful enough to dismantle,
patient enough to gnaw
but always bringing with it
the slew and swing of change.

Spare Room

The morning sun peers
hopefully through the window to
      touch
a small metropolis of packing boxes
nestled in the corner

So many memories are entombed
in these cardboard sepulchres,
      stagnant in darkness
while we manoeuvre our lives
(so seasoned here)
somewhere   else,

These conduits of pleasure,
once privy to the intimacies of our lives,
      propagators of our histories,
wait
like us,
to feel the rootedness of home,

though, perhaps I too am one
of these archival boxes,
lingering,
rigid

yearning to have purpose again.

After Rain

Raindrops loom
from the battery of our liquidambar's leaves,
poised and cool before
        diving
into the earthy void of the garden below

fronds of maidenhair,
                petal of rose,
hang lowly under the weight
of riding droplets and
the wind's cruel buffeting

winged creatures warble and frolic
in the damp of the lawn
        sifting through muddy bed for
earthy prize

It's unclear if the sun will pierce
this luminescent haze of white and grey
        with confident panes of gold and yellow

or if this momentary stillness
                is only the deep breath
                        before the second deluge.

First Snow, August 2014

Driving along this snake of road, and trees,
we are welcomed by an ethereal sprinkling,
        that falls
                mellifluously from its gathering perch,
in the bowers of canopy and branch.

Like a Friedrich painting, the crest becomes a bleached
mantle of gentle coldness:
        eucalypt and fern dusted in   virginal
        powder,
        beguiled,
like wedding guests or the New Year's Eve rabble,
        all come out to frolic in your majesty,
lulled and uplifted

You're not as I imagined you to be
a feathery grain that bites at my fingertips,
somehow reminding me that
what the cups of my palms
have caught,
asks to be returned.

When I leave you, I won't ever neglect
        your touch, this pallid aura,
those whispers of kisses on my skin,
so soft they might've been dreamt
        so real they won't be forgotten.

Beach at Night

When night comes   after the
enamelled beckoning of moon –
        scorch of white light washing
across the beach like a dam
whose bank is broken –
        an electric hum
                of creatures begin to promenade
to the clapping of surf
        on sand

it is companionable to step
into the pearled space,
        almost incantatory –
under a festooned sheet of velvet
brown and black,
I   the pilgrim
on this sacred plain.

Sitting at the glassy shore,
tang of salty air
        and spray
stirring my nostrils,
film of sand latching to my skin
soon to ossify

the ocean before me so fathomless,
        speckled skin wavering,
whispering to me   new things:
transcendental,
                sacral,
known only to the watching
moon.

The Lamplight of Our Existence

Earliest Morning

for some reason
I am awake through the illusory hours before dawn

a drape of mist swathes its smoky fabric
across the paddock – dense with quiet –
enveloping
each blade of grass
already embossed with crust of frost,
and the lonesome swing set
settled with dew

the kettle whistles with zeal
and promise –
I am drawn back into the warm
embrace of home and a fresh cup of coffee,

      to wait
      for protracted hours to
            depart,

                  drip

and fall away

            like a wall of morning ice.

Beehive

As a child I remember
the buttery hum
of gold and black jackets
        beneath the red gum banister,
making the home's inhabitants
and visitors unwilling
to cross the threshold, step
        near this volatile barrel
and seek retreat
inside;

Clustering on and over one another,
shepherding,
        filtering in
the hexagonal bower of hive –
so distressing

My eyes are fixed
by this panoply of sound and sight:
fear lurches
                rising;
I run inside.

Learning Oil Painting

Sumptuous curves,
        kaleidoscopic folds of paint
commingling across the vast landscape
of canvas,
open channel from mind to hand,
sense derived from style,
stroke

I sit at the white rectangle of possibility
                              before me –
fingers,
        indextrous and lacking
the surgical precision required,
to orchestrate a pool of tint and conduct
        rhythm   tonality   and   crescendo

potent movement,
        hue and tone fusing
under the lapping layers of paint,
the richness of potential
        rising in my increasingly
                confident hand.

Planting

the time has arrived for
        the churning of soil,
        the plotting of garden bed –
dust of last season's growing
has been cleared   and winter's ire
has been replaced
with days of sun and ease

the joy   the cosseting in
slipping
bulb and punnet of
plantlets
into vats of tilled earth

though now scant,
these infantile growers will –
under temperate sun and with sup
of water –
        burst
with a wink and flash   of colour,
becoming jewels
in our backyard

until next season's planting.

Dinner, Devour, Dachshund

Plating up the minced meat selection
I see that Pavlov was onto something:
this desperate mutt
hovering
at the brink of the food bowl –
caramel and onyx coat gleaming in fading sun –
squatting
     as far as his inordinately long body allows,
drooling as I assemble the platter
of fodder

only a moment later,
enough time for spoon to be placed in sink,
the tittering steps of the satisfied dachshund
  enters my house
off again to find some other venture,
      another salver of possibility.

Lost

I've lost it. I know I have.
                                                          But where?
Has it fallen
        from my frayed pocket,
(that I've long neglected to sew)
        slipped and   jumped
like a silvery fish
into the blackened embrace of irretrievable things?
        Or maybe
in my clammy hand
                it shot through an enthusiastic grasp
        ricocheting
somewhere
        bounding   hurtling like a red-eyed deer
in the shock
and proximity
        of headlights.

Gone.

Hospice

You asked if we could nurse you
in the solace of our household
carrying you through
the winter of your life,
away from ward and oncologist
and nauseating drugs,
wanting instead to feel the warmth and intimacies
of home.

I provisioned the guest room,
                looking out over lake and mangrove,
with small comforts,
though I wondered how
crisp sheets
and new pyjamas
could placate the impending
        cessation of breath
        the unknown space after death

I found you one night
sitting at the kitchen table
with a cup of tea (Mum exhausted in bed),
        hands shaking, fever surging through
the causeways of your body –
'Are you afraid?' I asked
'No,' you said

and I knew that it wasn't fear
or madness that grasped you
but the longing to be free
from the body that had
betrayed you,
to go
                            somewhere
filled with newness
like the onset sweeping of rain.

That Day, Winter '04

That day, winter '04. At the sea: nocuous green and turbulent, flecked with flashes of white. You and I are sitting at the cliff's edge, curtained by the high grass, like lions surveying gazelles. It will rain soon, but we won't go. We can't go back. The ocean air dances through your shirt; pirouettes of cologne exciting my nostrils. I want to touch you, you want to touch me. We both know it. Your eyes, mesmerising, search for something inside me. Something dormant and deep. Something that belongs in the ocean before us. Something I won't ever reveal.

Alone

I went searching
not knowing where to go,
but I went out nonetheless

the peppy galahs
were blotches of rose
on the pelt of the hill

I went searching in the rousing morning,
into the windings of my mind
swimming neural channels
glittering and doleful

attuned to the vibrations
of body and earth
then,
I was pulled back by the raucous
orchestra
of commuter traffic

shocked out of the blissful trance
of being alone.

Overawe

Your words
                    meanly shaped
cut and molested
his diffident
heart

there,
a wound
        enamelled,
there the boy,
                exposed
mocked,
abjured;
he worked hard,
patient,
continuing to   breathe,
dreams unrealised.

Then,
the pallor of the sun
turned his face
from a dark hurl of water:
                gently rising for
offerings of newness,
untrampled pastures.

Passing Through

no one ever
got close before

but you

are near enough
to intrude through

the holes in my skin
and dance across

the halls of my
heart. You've built

a settlement
in my mind

and I don't know
how to move you on

yet if you said
you were just

passing through I
don't think I could

go on.

Tenterhooks

no i know
this isn't going to end well –
even before it starts or something
like that
but i would like to say,
blind and unknowing,
that if my hand were only to brush
yours
i would know for a moment
what it is
to feel the thirst
to live.

Umbrella Bells

Fathoms below in the black abyss,
so far away
from the sunlit zone,
a spectre – otherworldly –
floats and shimmers,
        pulsing through the dark

spindly ribbons of thread
move through
the dusty grime,
bowl-like body emitting a strange luminescence,
inviting and repelling
its watery neighbours

confined to the blackness,
this creature from a dream
is a beautiful danger:
desired and feared
        and desperately

alone.

The Boy With Two Sugars in His Tea

there were dawns i could've
written for you and precipices i would've plunged from
so i wouldn't have to know hell,
so i'd never know parting
from you,
the boy with two sugars in his tea

four years ago
i'd made a life of not going into the sun
but i came out of silence into the
dangerous landscape of you,
the boy with two sugars in his tea

you took photos to capture beauty
absent from your life,
but i held everything about you
beautiful,
the boy with two sugars in his tea

you had that special something
spark, the paradox wrapped in
skinny jeans and flannel shirts,
the boy with two sugars in his tea

the things you'd tell me,
so many things,
it was nice to have someone
to talk to I said, and you agreed
and for a moment I wasn't in hell with
the boy with two sugars in his tea,

on the bus we listened to john mayer
you said you had a girlfriend
and i cared and i didn't
because i thought you'd still be mine,
the boy with two sugars in his tea

and maybe you loved me
and maybe you didn't
and maybe you didn't know,
the boy with two sugars in his tea

winter saw tears fall
in bathtubs and on pillows,
and all the while you asked
how did we go from kiss-chasy to killing ourselves?
the boy with two sugars in his tea

New Home

unfamiliar   to the music of our voices,
the cadence of our bodies,
our new home is an unprinted space
                              of wooden bone
                                           and plastered muscle

fatherly walls coloured in eggshell
await our conversations
over tea,
the arras of our daily lives:
making of beds
and harvesting of washing from the line

We are strangers, we are acquaintances
in this province of possibility.

Like arteries
these unauthored spaces are suffused
            with longing,
                                    lifeblood
coursing through
room to room
in the lamplight of our existence

this ecosystem we've come to inhabit,
            the tendril of our hope.

Lasik

Laser-assisted in situ keratomileusis

Red pulse
        of light
honing in on ocular trauma,
years' old veil removed,
rest,

splashes of saline, then
seeing,
        unaided.
Crisp and startling:
the serrated curve of leaf,
craggy skin of brick,

eyes open
to the endless recognition
of the world's beauty.

The Trembling Flame

Hummingbird

With copter flutter
the hummingbird lands on the oaken branch
        amidst a curtain of shrubbery

              head juddering,
sharp eyes scrutinising,
she dips from branch to twig
discerning the aptness of her prospective
settlement

with her long beak she deposits the spoils
        of her scavenges,
interlacing twig and grass,
lichen and web
with ardour,
caressing the infant home with her crest.

Hours are spent scavenging,
using winglet and breast to mould –
redo what the eddies of wind undo,
and by week's end
              the thatching will be made.

In the kettle of life where
ovules are laid,
the hummingbird puffs her feathers upon them
and waits,
forsaking herself and
relying now on the steadfastness of her
        making.

Depression, 2012

Waves came rolling
in sheets of foam and greyness,
and before I knew, my hapless body was
engulfed
in the ocean's violent embrace

it wasn't the cold,
                      but the rhythmic perpetuity
that got me:
inhibiting breath   and the belief
that there might be more
than this dark expanse of grey –
      (so close to black);

that I might one day emerge,
triumphant
                  from the cauldron of water
and feel warm clothes
      and the hues of the sun, but

there is no light here.
And the further
      I'm carried   out   by the brutal arms of ocean,
the less I think I will
or can
                be saved.

Fever

Somewhere in the warrens of my body
pathogens malign cell and system
        bringing to the surface
a violent swelter,
slur of words,
                and I am pinioned
                in some hallucinatory space
of abstract form
            and shadowy figures,
rising,
staggering,
then blackness

a moment of clarity and I
recognise the dialogue of ICU, an elapse of time,
                a ministry at my bedside,
and I'm swimming back into
the security of cognisance,
surfacing   like a diver
from the barrel of some dark and terrible water.

I Do Not Miss You

I do not miss you as the shore does the wash of the surf, or twigs do
their fallen leaves, or in front of others' eyes.
I miss you as a dialogue between soul and heart.

I miss you between the covers of a life put right
but broken where the dark flower of your thought grows;
I miss you as the question that goes unanswered and
the absence of words becomes daily.

I miss you with an indelible fever that surpasses logic,
a sickness that attacks deeper than body and
because of my love for you, I unravel.

I miss you as a fool, with hope and craving,
for I know that light cannot ward off the shadow
of your going   left here, I do not exist,
and half will only ever be whole.

Eyes

Heavy lidded with
sheath of skin
        creased;
I swim
        deeply in a
cerulean cascade,
eyes
sharp   sheets of membrane –
a flicker
seeing me
        knowing me:
your eyes.

Insomnia

        I stir in the bedroom's dark cataract,
house quiet with the lullaby
of somnolent hours –
the night's fire now ashen memory,
the hamlet settled in the hush
        of restfulness;

still, unease grips me,
        moves me,
my corking body unable to fall
into the slumbering channel –
annoyance
        activating my mind,
firing neuron   and thought

        What to do?
Write these thoughts down,
        exorcise this grief,
arise and iron today's shirt;
        beguile the hours' long passing.

Awake

The house is quiet. Only
the low humming of the fridge and the house's
creaking bones dent
the restful hush of night
(unheard by me while I sleep, swimming in boundless ocean)

a sudden bark
        through the quiet house and
I am lurched from dreaming,
body pulled and mangled,
my heart annexed by shock,
and fear –
the continuing surge of sound

the stasis of my slumberous mind is
sharply
disquieted, and like an eagle on the hunt
I dive
downstairs,
not knowing what I'll find,
        scouring rooms and pools of shadow,
                checking locks and appeasing dog

now I am awake.

Spider's Web

Climbing tightropes
of delicate hexagonal tapestry,
clutching desperately
from the crannies
of desiccated bark;

bobbling in the wind's soft rocking,
invisible   until
its threads glimmer with silver
        in the pulse of the
sun,

still – almost meditative –
she waits
        for the fools to get tangled
in her deathly architecture:
resigned,
regal;

though battered now from the wild north westerlies,
displaced from the tree's crackled skin,
her web has succeeded –
a bite!
        roused from fortitudinous,
                the spider's mottled body shifts,
moving quickly;
she will at last eat.

Rose and Thorn

Spines of light
slice through
the awning of green scrub in the garden, falling
on a contraposed bushel
       of spindly limbs

It rises from the fragrant coolness
of dirt
its mean shape an armoury
defending blooming pastel pillows

Tasting threads of vermilion,
I gather
perfumed ovaries –
of sumptuous creamy colour –
away from the familiarity of awning,
jagged leaf   blade of light
and speared stem,
swaddling hues of red, orange and yellow
in a rattan basket,
       with the riches of harvest.

Metamorphosis

A cocoon slings from a humble
branch in the backyard:
the presence within its furred crust
        busy
with the flurry of transformation

even so, all this possibility
– neatly parcelled and eagerly awaiting –
        is heartbreakingly close
to never becoming realised.
The sheathed miracle has no option
but resilience

despite ever-present danger
and uncertainty.

                How I wish I could be such a creature,
removed from the confines of ordinariness
to emerge
        resplendent, newly made –
a shadow of my former self

changed.

Tattoo

The needle is a maddened bird
drilling
        diving
                through the corporal pool of my body,

with each pulse my flesh sunders, becoming
impregnated,
skin and cell espousing the foreign liquid
swelling from within

reddened,
pain residual in the bowers of my mind,
I am wrapped
        and left to heal,

to wait
until this bloodied muddle is expunged by a jacket
of new skin.

Scars

are etched on the young field
of her skin:
musical notes from an unmelodic and arrhythmic
        score
read with gently hovering fingertips

across the depths and shallows
        of her body
(all her body)
are these white and jagged
        slices –
made not by the surgeon's careful
scalpel   but by violence,
desperate to live
                desperate to die

silenced behind the screen
of her clothes, she asks will I
be another star added to
        edging her even closer to heaven.

Hands

These hands before me
are beyond the skill
of Michelangelo
                or Bernini,
conduits of the love and pleasure that vibrates,
whinnies
          and quivers
in my body;

I have touched these hands –
your hands –
smooth like wave and smoke,
          sublime as an elusive
kudos;
fingers lined and ringed
               with time
that has shaped you, made you
enfolded me into the grain of you

               although capricious,
they might rise like birds
and after mile's journey, take rest
          on the cage of my chest.

Candle

Spark of phosphorus and
the trembling flame of the candle
cuts through
the dimness of the room:
        pirouettes of smoke ascend from wick,
flumes of wax
thick and molten,
drip and blob down the waffled barrel of beeswax

arbitrary paths of falling,
forming
biomorphic shapes
                comedic and haunting;
the flow of nature, the pull
of gravity
pooling on some cold and dimensional surface.

Beyond This

I do not know if there is something else,
some other
                 place
for the recently dead.

I like to think that
        beyond
our fleeting stretch of life,
our temporary case of skin and organ,
there is a Further   where Spirit might
endure

to where, I don't know
to what purpose, I can't say:

but if such a place does exist
I hope it would be like   passing
         from one room to another,
brief and modest –
a shift in climate and texture
enriched with a new point
                and purpose.

www.ingramcontent.com/pod-product-compliance
Lightning Source LLC
Chambersburg PA
CBHW062149100526
44589CB00014B/1759